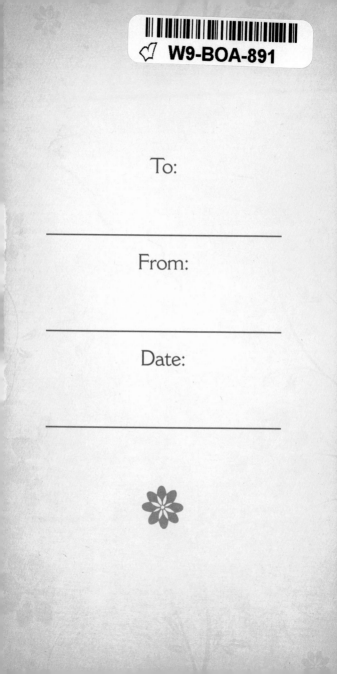

W9-BOA-891

To:

_____

From:

_____

Date:

_____

GodMoments
for
Moms

Carolyn Larsen

GodMoments for Moms

Copyright © 2012 Carolyn Larsen
All rights reserved.

Developed in co-operation with Educational Publishing
Concepts

© 2012 Christian Art Gifts, RSA
        Christian Art Gifts Inc., IL, USA

Designed by Christian Art Gifts

Images used under license from Shutterstock.com

Scripture quotations are taken from the *Holy Bible,* New
International Version® NIV®. Copyright © 1973, 1978, 1984, 2011
by International Bible Society. Used by permission of Zondervan
Publishing House. All rights reserved.

Printed in China

ISBN 978-1-77036-905-4

16 17 18 19 20 21 22 23 24 25 – 18 17 16 15 14 13 12 11 10 9

Introduction

Hey there,

I can just hear what you are thinking ... "My life is CRAZY busy. I cannot ... simply cannot add one more thing to my schedule. Sure, I want to spend time with God ... but WHEN?" Yes, I hear you and I'm right there with you.

We seem to live our lives on the proverbial hamster wheel and we make choices every day as to what we have time for and what we have to let go. But, the truth is that starting your day by spending a moment with God (if you only have a moment) will definitely make your day better.

So, take a few moments to focus your heart on the truth of His presence with you in every circumstance. Allow His love to guide you through this busy day in all you do and in all your relationships. A God Moment makes a God Day!

Controlled Speech

My teenager stomped out of the room ...
again ... angry with house rules and parental discipline
and more than happy to loudly announce her
frustration. I want to broadcast my own frustration
with her behavior just as loudly.

But I don't. Sometimes self-control is not fun.
However, it is the mature thing and I need to show
emotional and spiritual maturity. Shooting back an
angry response will just start a battle that could be
difficult to recover from.

Controlling my tongue can mean losing a battle
but winning the war.

*Remember not only to say the right thing
in the right place, but far more difficult still,
to leave unsaid the wrong thing at
the tempting moment.*
- Benjamin Franklin -

Top Priority

Big plans today ... dashed by a sick child. Instead of being at that important meeting, taking charge, sharing the plans I've worked so hard on and using my brain, I'm rocking my baby and humming lullabies. It seems that so often what I want to do is overpowered by what I need to do.

Sometimes I wonder if I'll ever have time to "be me" again. Am I to settle down to a life of diapers and baby food with being a soccer mom in my future? I once thought I could change the world and that is exactly what I want to do!

But here I am, reading to my child, playing with her, teaching her things, and yes, loving her with all my heart. Wait a minute ... maybe that is changing my world, my little corner of the world!

*I long to accomplish a great and noble task,
but it is my chief duty to accomplish small
tasks as if they were great and noble.*
- Helen Keller -

Walk the Talk

Follow my example,
as I follow the example of Christ.
- I Corinthians 11:1 -

We were in a hurry – as usual. Racing through the drive-thru of a fast food restaurant on our way to soccer practice. I grabbed the bag of food and the change and handed it all to my son so I could keep on going. "Mom," my son exclaimed, "that boy gave you $16.54 instead of just $6.54. Wow, we got our food and made money!"

I could have kept driving, after all we were running late. But, how many times have I talked with my son about the importance of honesty? Talk is cheap if actions don't match it. Right this minute I had a chance to show him what honesty looks like. I parked the van and ran inside to return the extra money. And my son saw me do it.

Don't worry that children never listen to you;
worry that they are always watching you.
- Robert Fulghum -

Time for Important Things

Above all, love each other deeply,
because love covers over a multitude of sins.
- 1 Peter 4:8 -

Time. There is never enough of it. Seriously, how can I be so out of shape when I spend so much energy dashing from one place to another? I know I'm over-committed but I don't know what to cut out of my schedule. The things I'm busy with are good things that are worthy of my time.

However, there are only 24 hours in a day so when I fill my waking hours with responsibilities: my most important responsibilities get pushed aside, my children. Then, in guilt I toss a new toy or some special dinner at them to show them how very much I love them.

My priorities are upside down. I pray for God's help to get them straight so my first priority (after God, of course) is to spend good, quality time with my children. That is the only thing that will show them how much I truly love them.

In bringing up children, spend on them half
as much money and twice as much time.

- Anonymous -

Taking Control

Whoever loves discipline loves knowledge,
but he who hates correction is stupid.
- Proverbs 12:1 -

"Bedtime!" I call to my kids. Their response, as always, "Just a minute!" Big sigh — I should put my foot down and insist that they obey, but ... discipline takes so much energy.

Enforcing rules makes my children angry and that takes even more energy to work through. Of course rules are made to protect my children, keep them healthy and help them become responsible adults. I know that. I also know that God has rules for me (well, for all of us) and that following those rules teaches me to become a better Christ-follower.

So, I guess rules are important and that putting my foot down and insisting on obedience is good for my children in the long run. I can put up with an unhappy child for the short-term in order to grow a responsible, productive adult in the long run.

Parents who are afraid to put their foot down
usually have children who step on their toes.
- Chinese Proverb -

Words Well Spoken

*Do not let any unwholesome talk
come out of your mouths, but only
what is helpful for building others up.*
- Ephesians 4:29 -

Encouraging words lift my spirits. In the dark moments of a bad day my thoughts often slide back to some compliment given — even if from a long time ago. It makes me feel good to remember that at least at one point, someone liked something I did.

Now that I think about it, the same is probably true of my children. My compliments and encouraging words make them feel better about who they are.

Wow, I've got to be careful that my words to them are not constantly complaints or criticisms. I don't want to tear them down, I want to build them up. I must notice the good things they do and affirm those. I'm guessing that those words will bring more good behavior that encourages more positive statements. Good words beget good behavior.

*Speak a word of affirmation at the right
moment in a child's life and it's like lighting
up a whole roomful of possibilities.*
- Gary Smalley -

Respect
Begets Respect

"I will not allow you to speak to me that way. I'm your mother. You will respect me!" I FIRMLY tell my daughter. Then I realize that when someone "demands" something of me my hackles (what is a hackle anyway?) go up and I want to strongly resist.

I know it isn't right. I'm working on it. But, as I think about my own reaction to demands, I become aware of how my children may feel when I demand respect and civil treatment from them. It makes sense that respect must be earned by how I treat them, which hopefully is with respect. My hackles are also activated when my children speak rudely to me, or worse, refuse to speak to me at all. Yet, I am reminded to speak civilly and respectfully to them — to treat them as I would like to be treated.

How else will they learn to treat others with respect?

Don't demand respect as a parent.
Demand civility and insist on honesty.
But respect is something you must earn —
with kids as well as with adults.
- William Attwood -

Bedtime Habits

Bedtime ... finally. It's been a tough day. In fact, a couple of times I wondered about resigning from motherhood. My children were constantly and consciously disobedient; arguing and fighting with one another, testing the boundaries of what they know is allowed ... not fun to be around. I'm actually relieved to put them to bed and have a little peace in what's left of my day.

But later when I peek into their rooms and see their angelic faces as they sleep, I'm overwhelmed with love for them. I realize that this day was probably as difficult for them as it was for me. I tiptoe into their rooms and plant gentle kisses on those soft little cheeks and thank God for the privilege of being their mom.

I ask Him to help me be a better mom tomorrow — more patient and perhaps more creative so that we may have a happier day together. I love them so much.

Always kiss your children goodnight —
even if they're already asleep.
- H. Jackson Brown, Jr. -

Busy Is Best

"There's nothing to do," my teenager whines as I'm scrubbing the floor and my mental to-do list is growing longer and longer. I'm not very sympathetic to her boredom.

I offer to give her some "things" to do. But for some reason, those things do not interest her. It seems fair to ask her help with work around the house. After all, she lives here, too. Apparently it doesn't seem fair to her. She feels her boredom should be solved by a trip to the mall with her friend.

However, I remember my own mother's declaration that "idle hands are the devil's workshop" and that keeping teens busy keeps them out of trouble. (No, I didn't agree with her when I was a teen.) I know that as my daughter learns to help with things around the house she is learning to take care of herself and therefore live independent from Mom one day. So ... here's the chore list, Honey!

*Work spares us from three evils:
boredom, vice, and need.*
- Voltaire -

Admitting I'm Wrong

You then, my son, be strong in
the grace that is in Christ Jesus.
- 2 Timothy 2:1 -

I wish there was an instruction manual for parents. I fear that I mess up way too often. I don't want to ruin my children. One of the hardest things I've had to learn is to admit when I'm wrong. There have been times when I've put my foot down and made a non-negotiable decision only to realize later that I was wrong. It's difficult then to say, "I'm sorry. I was wrong. Will you forgive me?" I suppose it makes me feel weak or something.

I have to believe though that modeling the humility of this action will only help my children. As they see and experience my graciousness in admitting mistakes, and my quiet humility when I'm right, they will hopefully learn these skills, too. I know this is an important thing to teach my children, just as it's important for me to learn. Grace. Always behave with grace.

Where we are wrong, make us willing
to change, and where we are right,
make us easy to live with.
- Peter Marshall -

A Step at a Time

*Perseverance must finish its work so that you may
be mature and complete, not lacking anything.*
- James 1:4 -

My son has a huge project due at school. He's
had plenty of time to work on it but seems to sit
and stare at the computer screen and ... accomplish
nothing. The project seems so big to him that he
doesn't know where to start. I'm slightly annoyed
with him because I don't want to have to pull an all-
nighter with him the night before the project is due.

"Just get started," I tell him impatiently. But then
I realize how I'm behaving toward the big Mother/
Daughter Retreat I'm in charge of. I'm not sure
where to start with this massive responsibility so ... I
do nothing. Yeah, same thing.

We will work together to break down our projects
into bite-sized daily portions that are manageable.
Then, slowly, a step at a time, our work will be done
and we will have both learned important lessons
about tackling big jobs!

To climb steep hills requires a slow pace at first.
- William Shakespeare -

Making Memories

*Our mouths were filled with laughter, our tongues
with songs of joy. Then it was said among the nations,
"The Lord has done great things for them."*
- Psalm 126:2 -

When dinner is over my family immediately scatters. Husband, children, even the family dog gives up his begging and heads outside with the kids.

Sometimes, while I'm scraping and rinsing the dishes before loading the dishwasher, I hear all of them playing outside and I'm a little bit resentful. I want to play, too. I'm so task-oriented that I can't let myself leave the dishes for later while I go outside to play.

When I hear my ten-year-old son come in the house, something in my task-oriented brain breaks loose and as he walks through the kitchen, I grab the sprayer hose from the sink and squirt him right in the face. He looks absolutely shocked so ... I spray him again. Pretty soon we're wrestling over the sprayer, sliding on the wet floor and ... making a memory that neither of us will ever forget.

*Each day of our lives we make deposits
in the memory banks of our children.*
- Charles R. Swindoll -

Undivided Attention

This is the confidence we have in approaching God:
that if we ask anything according to His will,
He hears us.
- 1 John 5:14 -

"Momma, momma, momma!" Remember how eagerly you anticipated your toddler learning to speak? Did you used to hang on every sound she made and try with all your might to turn the mumbles into "Momma?" Then when her words came, you celebrated, right? You laughed at every cute little saying she came up with and especially the words she made up when she didn't know the correct word. Aaaah yes, so cute.

The thing is that once children learn to talk, many of them NEVER stop talking. In order to stay sane and actually get anything done, you learn to tune out the constant chatter coming from your toddler. That's understandable. However, there are times when your child needs to know that she has your undivided attention and that you are listening to every word she utters. That shows your care.

In a similar way, aren't you glad to know that you have God's undivided attention when you talk with Him?

Love is giving someone your undivided attention.
- Anonymous -

Battling Anger

Refrain from anger and turn from wrath;
do not fret – it leads only to evil.
- Psalm 37:8 -

I wonder if the tendency to have a quick temper that hangs on to anger is hereditary. Anger is something I've struggled with my whole life. When I was younger and got angry with a sibling or a friend, I held on to that anger and fed it until it consumed me. Sometimes I got so busy being angry that I forgot why I was angry. I've worked on this issue for years and prayed for God's help in overcoming it.

When I see similar anger issues in my child, it saddens my heart. I know that many of my relationships were damaged or even ended because of my anger issues. I don't want my child to have to go through that pain. I pray for the right words spoken at the right moment to share with her the lessons I've learned. I pray for her open heart to hear and for God to work in making her own heart tender and more forgiving so that she won't have the same struggles I've had.

Anger is often more hurtful than
the injury that caused it.
- English Proverb -

Strength Builder

God is our refuge and strength,
an ever-present help in trouble.
- Psalm 46:1 -

"Mommy, I'm scared." I pull my young son into my arms and hold him tightly. I love being needed, but I'm sad that he is scared. What a privilege I have to teach him to pray through his fear. He learns to ask God to walk with him each step of the way. I stay alongside him as much as possible as he faces things that scares him ... and gets through it.

He gains faith and trust in God in a practical way. He gains confidence in himself so that the next time something frightens him, he won't shake quite so much. He will be able to look back at this experience and see that he made it through and then believe that he can do it again.

You gain strength, courage and confidence
by every experience in which you
really stop to look fear in the face.
- Eleanor Roosevelt -

A World View

I want my child to have a worldview. I long for him to know there are people in this world with different skin colors, different economic conditions, different religions and different beliefs.

I want him to understand how big the world is and that boys and girls on the other side of the planet are his brothers and sisters because God made them too.

I pray for God to help me effectively teach him to love those around him, even the ones who are different and to love those far away. We are all made in God's image.

True Contentment

I know what it is to be in need, and I know what it is to have plenty. I have learned the secret of being content in any and every situation, whether well fed or hungry, whether living in plenty or in want.

- Philippians 4:12 -

My son constantly asks for more ... toys, restaurants and vacations. We live in a time of "more." The media and the world around us bombard us with ads showing things they want us to believe we absolutely must own. Consequently, it is a battle to ever be satisfied with what we have. How do I protect my children from the attitude of "Give me more and more and more"? I will remind them of what they do have and the inequity of those things compared with people who don't have even the basics of life.

I pray that God will teach my children (and OK, me too) to be content with what we have and to not always be looking for more. I pray that we will know the contentment of being satisfied and the joy of giving to others. Help us all, dear God, to be thankful for what we have.

He who desires is always poor.

- Claudianus -

The Company You Keep

Don't let anyone look down on you because you are young, but set an example for the believers in speech, in life, in love, in faith and in purity.
- 1 Timothy 4:12 -

"You're known by the company you keep." My parents used to say that to me. I didn't want to hear it because I didn't want to give up any of my friends. Now I understand these words so well. I have the wisdom of my years and the perspective of a parent: A parent who sees her teenager hanging around with some kids who do not make good choices and who are pulling my child down with them.

Sure, it's OK to be friends with kids who need a Christian example. The danger comes when their actions slide into my son's life, too. It's easy to get so used to something that it suddenly seems like an acceptable way of life. Then, he gets lumped in with kids who are rebellious, dishonest or unkind. He is judged by their actions and even his stand as a Christ-follower is damaged.

When the character of a man is not clear to you, look at his friends.
- Japanese Proverb -

Disciplined!

My son, do not despise the LORD's discipline and do not resent His rebuke, because the LORD disciplines those He loves, as a father the son he delights in.
- Proverbs 3:11-12 -

One of my TV-watching memories goes back to the program *Happy Days* when the gang was gathered in the diner but no one could get the juke box to play music. Fonzie always saved the day by coming up and hitting the box in exactly the right place. The music would pop on and all was well. Sometimes people are like that, too — people of all ages.

We need that pop that sends us into action. That most often comes from God Himself but sometimes He uses people to be the motivators. Sometimes He uses moms. I just pray that He keeps me balanced between the pats on the backs for my kids and the little pop that gets them moving.

And ... may those pops always be done in love, not anger.

*We all need a pat on the back sometimes;
and occasionally some of us need
a boot on the seat of our pants.*
- Anonymous -

The Want Muscle

*Set your minds on things above,
not on earthly things.*
- Colossians 3:2 -

It's hard for kids not to want everything their friends have. Who am I kidding? It's hard for me sometimes, too. If I let my "want muscle" run wild I start wanting everything from big screen TVs to expensive shoes and fancy cars. Fine things but not necessities. I see that in my children, too.

They see the gadgets, toys, designer clothes and amazing vacations their friends or classmates get and they want the same. One of my sons nearly drove me insane over a certain kind of basketball shoes — the kind we can't afford.

It's a good reminder that happiness never comes from things. Often, the more a person has the more she wants — that want muscle is never satisfied. So, we are constantly learning to set our affections on things above; the things that have the real value of loving and serving God.

*Before you set your heart on something,
look around you to see how happy
people are who have it.*
- Anonymous -

Lessons from Tough Times

The Lord God is a sun and shield;
the Lord bestows favor and honor;
no good thing does He withhold
from those whose walk is blameless.
- Psalm 84:11 -

Life Lesson #2,653 ... maturity shows when you find ways to make the best of a difficult situation. Well, that may not be the correct Life Lesson number, however, it is an important lesson and one that proves difficult for children to learn.

When my daughter tried out for the basketball team and didn't make it ... again, it was time to work on this life lesson. The girl has tried out for every sport her school offers and made none of them. Instead of letting her sink to the depths of depression, we talked about how she could use her free time to focus on other things she enjoys — like drama.

Sure enough, next time there were play auditions, she was right there. She didn't get the lead, but she did get a part! It was a good lesson for her (and for me) to look for the opportunities that disappointments afford.

When the best things are not possible,
the best may be made of those that are.
- Richard Hooker -

Earning What You Want

A greedy man stirs up dissension,
but he who trusts in the Lord will prosper.
- Proverbs 28:25 -

I don't know much about pigs but I do know about boys. I know from experience that a boy who gets everything he wants learns to think that rules will be changed to make his life more comfortable. Consequently, he doesn't obey any rules that are unappealing to him. A young man who gets every toy he wants is never satisfied. He will take the new one, look at it briefly then begin demanding the next one. He always wants more than what he has.

A boy who gets everything he wants does not know what it means to want and so can't identify with those who always want. Of course, this all applies to not just boys, but also to girls, moms, dads ... pretty much humans in general. We need to learn to work for the things we have. We appreciate things much more when we've earned them and waited to have them. All of us.

If you give a pig and a boy everything they want,
you'll get a good pig and a bad boy.
- Jackson Brown, Jr -

Standing Strong

*Be strong and courageous. Do not be afraid or terrified
because of them, for the Lord your God goes with you;
He will never leave you nor forsake you.*
- Deuteronomy 31:6 -

Backbone. I want my children to have the
backbone to stand up for themselves when necessary;
to stand up for others when necessary; to take the
high road; to be persistent. There are people in this
world who seem to be pushed every which way by
those who are stronger. It appears that these weaker
folks do not think for themselves or have the strength
to voice their own opinion. They are beaten into the
ground.

Then there are those who do the beating; those
who push others around and force their own will
and way on all. There must be a happy medium —
there must be those who stand up for themselves but
are also considerate and kind to others. That's how
I want to be and the way I pray my children will be.

Strong ... and kind ... Christlike.

*In this world a man must either
be an anvil or hammer.*
- Henry W. Longfellow -

Wading through Hard Times

*Do not fear, for I am with you; do not be dismayed, for
I am your God. I will strengthen you and help you;
I will uphold you with My righteous right hand.*
- Isaiah 41:10 -

I admit it. I try to fix my children's problems.
When I see them suffering or troubled by a situation or
problem I just want to solve it for them. From problems
at school to relationship issues to self-esteem problems —
I don't want them to be in pain. I want their lives to
be easy. In my mind, this behavior has just felt like a
mother's love in action.

However, the reality is that I'm not doing my
children any favors by my actions. By denying them
the difficulties of life, I'm keeping them from learning one of the most important lessons in life.

My children will only learn how to handle
problems and work through them by actually going
through the problems. I can walk alongside them,
giving advice when asked. I can pray for them and
remind them of God's presence and incredible love
for them. But, I must let them go through problems,
not around or over ... through them.

The best way out is always through.
- Robert Frost -

Time Wise

"Mom, I'm just about to reach the next level!" my videogame-playing son whines. I just want him to do his homework — how unreasonable of me!

Our modern, technological world is filled with gadgets that are hyped as absolutely necessary and incredible timesavers. However, it appears that these timesavers can actually be timewasters. How much time do you see your kids wasting on video games, social networks or texting? It's easier to waste time and put off doing work that needs to be done than ever before in history.

One of our jobs as moms is to teach our children to set priorities and stick to them; to encourage them to get their work taken care of before any down time activities. We can set an example of just that kind of behavior. God has given us only so many hours on this earth and using them wisely is a gift back to Him.

Dost thou love life?
Then do not squander time,
for that is the stuff life is made of.
- Benjamin Franklin -

Dream Big

We have different gifts, according to the grace given us. If a man's gift is prophesying, let him use it in proportion to his faith.
- Romans 12:6 -

What do your children dream of doing one day? Do you try to influence those dreams? One of my children wanted to grow up to be a grocery store checker and my tendency was to encourage bigger dreams. But really, is it more honorable to be a teacher or a garbage man? Do you secretly look down on some professions and elevate others?

If you do, you are likely passing that prejudice on to your children. If you believe that God has a purpose for every person on earth, then how can you secretly dismiss any job? Are you grateful to those who do the jobs you can't or wouldn't like to do? Do you appreciate those servants who make your life easier, safer or cleaner?

Dignity comes from a job well done — regardless of what the job is. Teach your children that and give them the freedom to do whatever work they are gifted at and interested in. Celebrate what God has called them to.

No race can prosper till it learns that there is as much dignity in tilling a field as in writing a poem.
- Booker T. Washington -

God's Artwork

*Let us consider how we may spur one
another on toward love and good deeds.*
- Hebrews 10:24 -

What fun it is to praise my daughter for a job
well done! Praise is so important. From the time
children are very young and just testing the waters in
so many areas, praise is what will keep them moving
forward. When your child wants to clear the dinner
table, are you satisfied with the job she does and do
you praise her work? Or do you feel the need to go
behind her and improve on her work? When your son
wants to audition for a solo in his school program,
do you praise his interest in the arts?

Do you celebrate your child's interest in sports,
collecting stamps or any other hobby, even if it
doesn't interest you? Can you encourage your child's
compassionate heart and yearning to help those less
fortunate than her? Our children are blank canvasses
and God is painting the details of their lives.

As their very important mother, your encou-
ragement and praise plays an important role in that
process.

Praise your children and they will blossom!

- Anonymous -

Lead with the Heart

*"Be merciful,
just as your Father is merciful."*
- Luke 6:36 -

Busy, busy, busy ... no time for sipping coffee with a friend or enjoying ice cream with my son. A task-oriented woman is often ruled by her mental to-do lists. There's nothing wrong with being task-oriented. In fact, thank the Lord for those people who get so very much done. Those of us who are not task-oriented, depend on those "doers"! But, for a mom, it is important to let items of the heart interrupt the to-do list once in a while.

Jesus is a model of this. How often was He interrupted by someone who needed His help? He always stopped, helped the person before Him and then went on His way. His heart was present with those who were with Him. His model is good ... get your work done ... stay focused ... but not at the expense of times when your children need you. Lead with your heart when necessary.

*A good rule for going through life is to
keep the heart a little softer than the head.*

- Anonymous -

Growing God's Child

*Being confident of this, that He who began
a good work in you will carry it on to
completion until the day of Christ Jesus.*
- Philippians 1:6 -

One of the most rewarding experiences of being a mother happens when you see your children start to blossom into the adults they will become. Young children often explore a lot of different interests and try many different things. That's part of the process of learning who God has created them to be. But, as they grow older, children focus on the things they enjoy and where they show aptitude.

It's not unusual for parents to first notice those talents before the children sort them out. What joy to discover, encourage, challenge and even help train your child to use those abilities and talents. The negative happens when a mom tries to push a child into being or doing what she always wanted to do — living vicariously through the child. Keep an open mind, keep seeing eyes, encourage your child to be the person God has made him or her to be!

*It is a fine thing to have ability, but the ability
to discover ability in others is the true test.*
- Elbert Hubbard -

The Important Stuff

*Each one should use whatever gift he has
received to serve others, faithfully administering
God's grace in its various forms.*
- 1 Peter 4:10 -

Making a living is a lot of work, isn't it? The cost of living and raising children increases all the time. Of course, the standard of what is a "nice life" is always growing larger, too, as well as the "stuff" we feel we need to have. Things that used to be luxuries have subtly become necessities. That keeps us working. In fact, it often keeps both Mom and Dad working.

Of course, there's nothing wrong with working or with teaching our children to work hard. However, it's important to remember that the stuff we get by working — the things we buy for ourselves and our children — those aren't what make a life. Our lives are blessed, enhanced and enjoyed by the time we spend together as a family and by the ways we teach our children to look around and see how they can bless, encourage and help others. Giving ... that's what makes our lives good.

*We make a living by what we get,
we make a life by what we give.*
- Sir Winston Churchill -

Green-Eyed Envy

A heart at peace gives life to the body,
but envy rots the bones.
- Proverbs 14:30 -

Why does it often seem that there is one kid who gets everything? Star athlete, lead in the plays, good grades, teacher's favorite ... and on top of it all a nice kid! Envy is a difficult emotion to get a handle on and yes, it takes a very pure heart to celebrate a friend's success without envy. That's especially hard when the success is in an area that your child desires to succeed in — but doesn't. How do you help your children learn to sincerely celebrate a friend's success without struggling through envy? Let's be honest, sometimes it's a life-long learning curve.

One place to start is with the reminder that God makes each of us unique. He has a plan for each person's life and will work out that plan in His own timeframe. When a friend succeeds at something it means God is working, so celebrate! And ... know that your turn will come ... in God's time.

When your child (and you!) understand this, it's a little easier to skip the envy path. Trust God's plan!

It is in the character of very few men to honor
without envy a friend who has prospered.

- Aeschylus -

Crowd Effect

In your anger do not sin;
when you are on your beds,
search your hearts and be silent.
- Psalm 4:4 -

I heard my daughter and her friends verbally ripping apart a girl from their class. Anger and criticism flowed freely through my mini-van. Friends are usually a wonderful group of people who support and encourage us through life. However, there is one dynamic of friendship to be wary of. That is the "herd effect" of anger. If your son or daughter is angry at someone and vents about it to friends, then the friends join in and feed the anger ... well, no good is going to come of that.

Anger that is fed and encouraged grows into bigger anger. Encourage your children to avoid that. Encourage them to diffuse the "herd effect" of anger by not joining in themselves. One good way to overcome anger is to pray for the person you're angry with. It's pretty hard to pray for someone and stay angry at them, too!

If you do not wish to be prone to anger,
do not feed the habit; give it nothing
which may tend to its increase.
- Epictetus -

Value Values

Unfortunately, the world and the media have turned the definition of success upside down. Success by the world's standards is defined by power, fame and money. The more a person has of those three things, the more successful he or she is deemed to be. With those "values" being blasted into your children's minds every day you will be fighting an uphill battle to recalculate their definition of success and cement that in their hearts.

Of course, God's Word gives a very clear definition of success so you have a handbook to work from. True success is becoming the person God intends you to be and displaying honesty, integrity, compassion and love in the process. True success has nothing to do with power, fame or money and in fact, may land a person in a place that is the opposite of all of those. But, success by God's definition makes a person of value to God, others and self!

Try not to become a man of success but a man of value.
- Albert Einstein -

Liking Me

Before I formed you in the womb I knew you,
before you were born I set you apart;
I appointed you as a prophet to the nations.
- Jeremiah 1:5 -

The statement below by one of America's most famous first ladies seems so obvious and so simple and yet it's sometimes so hard to put into practice — especially as children arrive at the middle school years.

It takes a pretty secure young teen to actually say he or she likes who they are. However, you, Mom, can help with this security a lot. Encouraging creativity and varied interests and complimenting successes helps a child like herself and who she is becoming.

Discouraging comparisons — even to siblings — is important, too. Remind your son or daughter that liking self is not pride but is acceptance of how God made them and that acceptance will help them to be better friends to those around them.

And then, just a question, Mom — can they see that modeled in you? Are you friends with who you are and how God made you?

Friendship with oneself is all-important,
because without it one cannot be
friends with anyone else in the world.
- Eleanor Roosevelt -

Living on the Edge

The eternal God is your refuge, and underneath are the everlasting arms. He will drive out your enemy before you, saying, "Destroy him!"
- Deuteronomy 33:27 -

Are you an "in-the-box" kind of person? Do you live your life safely and shy away from risks? Do you do things in the same pattern day after day? Do you have well-worn ruts in your life?

OK, it's not smart to do things that are just downright dangerous for no reason. But, if God offers to mix up your life a bit and give you some adventure, will you be up for it? Perhaps a bigger question is, "If God offers some adventure to your children, will you be up for that?" Will you encourage them to take hold of the opportunity?

Remember that God will not send your kids anywhere or ask them to do anything without walking along right beside them. Have you ever wondered about your own life if you've missed the opportunity to be a part of God's exciting work just because you were afraid of the adventure? Encourage your children to take risks when God opens doors.

Life is either a daring adventure or nothing.
- Helen Keller -

Safe at Home

All of you, live in harmony with one another;
be sympathetic, love as brothers,
be compassionate and humble.
- 1 Peter 3:8 -

Home ... where we can all be ourselves. That's a good thing and sometimes a difficult thing. Perhaps you've observed selfishness, anger, impatience, rudeness and lack of compassion that is sometimes displayed between siblings at home.

Have you feared that those same characteristics are displayed at school or other "outside the house" places? Hopefully you've been assured that your children are just fine in the classroom and with friends. So, why do those emotions pop out at home? Probably because it's a safe place — after all, family has to love a person, right?

A good reminder for parents and children alike is that family is always a part of life. So, building good relationships, even at a young age, is a good idea. Home is also a good place to learn to work through relationship problems and how to handle them with grace, love and compassion. Forgiveness, charity and love begin at home.

Charity begins at home.
- Terence -

Honoring God

*It is written: "As surely as I live," says the Lord,
"every knee will bow before Me;
every tongue will confess to God."*
- Romans 14:11 -

Have a look at the statement by A. W. Tozer below. Sometimes it's hard for a mother to admit that anything is more important to her than her love for her children. However, when you think about it, what you believe about God plays an important role in your love for your children. So, step back mentally and emotionally for just a moment and think about this statement.

What do you believe about who God is? Is living for Him, obeying Him, knowing more about Him, serving Him, growing in faith and trust important to you? For a mom of faith, those are all important decisions and putting God first in your life will only make you a better woman, better wife and better mom. Living out your faith honestly will be a testimony to and training ground for your children to know Him with that same intimacy.

*What we believe about God is the
most important thing about us.*
- A. W. Tozer -

Giving Up Worry

*"Do not worry about your life, what you will eat
or drink; or about your body, what you will wear.
Is not life more important than food,
and the body more important than clothes?"*
- Matthew 6:25 -

Are you a worrier? These scary economic times make worry a bit more prevalent than it used to be. With people losing jobs and homes, even the basics of food and clothing are harder to come by for regular people.

Of course, the words of the Bible encourage us not to worry because God will take care of us. After all, He takes care of the birds in the sky and the flowers in the field and they don't worry.

However, it's also good to remember that if God has blessed you with a body and brain that work, you should do what you can to take care of yourself and not expect Him to toss food your way while you lounge around eating bonbons and watching TV. This is a good thing to teach your children, too.

Use the resources God has given you to take care of yourself. Trust Him for the times you can't.

*God gives every bird its food,
but He does not throw it into its nest.*
- J. G. Holland -

Always Learning

If any of you lacks wisdom, he should ask God,
who gives generously to all without finding fault,
and it will be given to him.
- James 1:5 -

How boring life would be if you knew everything, right? There would be no new discoveries because there would be nothing left to learn. You have possibly met people who think they know everything about everything. Those people aren't much fun to be around, are they? It's interesting to think about how the understanding that all people still have something to learn applies to parenting. While moms have the benefit of experience from their own childhood and from being older, there are still things to learn.

Children today live in a different world because of the growth of social media and the Internet. Knowledge is different, opportunities are different and temptations are different.

A wise mom understands this and learns from it. Allow God to teach you about the world you and your children live in and how He desires you to parent your children and teach them to live and serve Him in it.

The wisest mind has something yet to learn.
- George Santayana -

Peaceful Living

Do not repay anyone evil for evil.
Be careful to do what is right in the eyes of everybody.
- Romans 12:17 -

Not many people enjoy confrontation. It's scary to "put yourself out there" and approach someone who openly disagrees with you or dislikes you. But, it's also not fun to know that there are people who feel that way about you. When you have an "enemy" do you make efforts to avoid her or keep necessary conversations short before walking away? Ignoring the problem will never solve it.

The only way to settle a difference is to talk with the person with whom you have the problem. Talking around it to others will not solve it. An honest, respectful conversation is the only direct approach that will help make peace. This is a good thing to remember for moms, too.

When you have differences with your children, respectfully discuss them, listening to your children's feelings and opinions. You still get to make decisions because you are the parent, but give them a chance to be heard.

If you want to make peace, you don't talk
to your friends. You talk to your enemies.

- Moshe Dayan -

Faith Walking

The Lord will guide you always;
He will satisfy your needs in a sun-scorched land
and will strengthen your frame.
- Isaiah 58:11 -

Learning to live life completely trusting God is a journey. Having enough faith to take the first step on a path God leads you to is pretty scary because you may not know where the second step will take you.

How do you help your children learn to live by faith rather than needing to see the spreadsheet of where their entire lives will go? The best way is by example. Do your children see you trusting God and His plan for you, even in the darkness of the unknown?

It's one thing to hear you say that you have faith in God, it's another to see it modeled in your life. Let your children see, not just the faith by which you live, but also the struggle to live out that faith sometimes. Through watching your journey they will learn how to make their own. Let them see that you believe God is the Waymaker for you and that even in your moments of weakness, you do believe that you can trust His path for you.

Faith is taking the first step even when
you don't see the whole staircase.
- Martin Luther King, Jr -

Kindly Speaking

A word aptly spoken is like apples
of gold in settings of silver.
- Proverbs 25:11 -

"Sticks and stones may break my bones but words will never harm me." Yeah, we know that old proverb is NOT true, don't we? Hurtful words linger in your mind and heart for a long time. Girls in middle school are especially capable of speaking words that bruise hearts for a long, long time. Those bruises are inside and therefore not obvious to others. Why is it that one mean word lays on the heart twice as long as twenty kind words?

Gently remind your children (boys and girls) that words, tone of voice and attitude can make a big difference in another person's life. Kind words encourage, lift up and motivate and their effect lasts a long time. Encourage them to measure their words and speak to others as they would like to be spoken to. Model this kind of speech for them and see their confidence and compassion for others blossom because of it.

Kind words can be short and easy to speak;
but their echoes are truly endless.
- Mother Teresa -

Family Life

He has made everything beautiful in its time.
He has also set eternity in the hearts of men;
yet they cannot fathom what God
has done from beginning to end.
- Ecclesiastes 3:11 -

True confession ... I thought I was doing the right thing by serving on every church committee that asked. It seemed to me that I was modeling capable, strong womanhood by leading two Bible studies. It never occurred to me that I was relegating my family to 4th or 9th place on my list of priorities.

Then one day I read a paper my daughter wrote for school. She described how her mom (that's me) was "so important" because I was out every night at meetings and doing things. She even quietly wrote that she missed spending time with me. Aaaah ... arrows in the heart.

Moms, there is absolutely nothing wrong with being involved in church work or committees or anything else. But, don't ever neglect time with your children for those things. Kids grow up so fast — be there to enjoy it.

The family was ordained by God before
He established any other institution,
even before He established the church.
- Billy Graham -

Time Management

I once heard a comedian recall how his mom used to say, "I only have two hands." Her statement made him think that his mom was physically challenged because other moms must have more than two hands.

I have often thought that perhaps God didn't think things through because it makes sense to me that for every child a woman has she should be given another arm as well. Good idea, right? OK, I'll admit that it would be hard to buy clothes.

It just always seems that there is not enough time to do the things on my daily to-do list. The reality is that I put things on that list that do not really need to be there. God gives me 24 hours in a day and when He gives me something to do, He gives me time to do it. It's my priorities that get skewed sometimes and that make my days so crazy.

So, Moms, let's get our priorities straight and do the important things!

God never imposes a duty
without giving the time to do it.
- John Ruskin -

Take a Stand

Blessed is the man who trusts in the Lord,
whose confidence is in Him.
- Jeremiah 17:7 -

When my daughters were young, one of them was definitely her own person. She didn't care about what others thought of her. She had her viewpoints and beliefs and she stood strong for them. My other daughter wanted everyone to like her. The scary danger was that she didn't stand for anything. She could be swayed to join in with whatever group she was with. I spent a lot of time in prayer for that girl. God answered those prayers and she is a strong woman of God now.

This is a good lesson to pass along to your children. Everyone will not always like you or agree with you. Rather than worrying about that, it's better to know what you believe and then stand for it. Otherwise you will get knocked down by people on both sides of the belief you are trying to avoid taking a stand for! Believe God and His Word and don't worry about those who disagree with you.

Standing in the middle of the road
is very dangerous. You get knocked
down by traffic from both sides.
- Margaret Thatcher -

Teachable Hearts

Do not be anxious about anything,
but in everything, by prayer and petition,
with thanksgiving, present your requests to God.
- Philippians 4:6 -

We try to teach our children about life. We try to protect them from dangerous things that could hurt them. We try to share the wisdom of our experience. When they are young, our children think Mom and Dad are experts at everything. They believe we have all the answers. But as they grow, children often test the limits and stretch for the opportunity to try their own hands at deciding what is best for their lives.

It's hard for a mom to watch these tests because we do not ever want our children to be hurt or be in danger. However, the fact is that sometimes experience is what teaches our kids the lessons we've told them about. So, pray that your children will have teachable hearts. Pray that the experiences they have will not be dangerous or harmful but will be only severe enough that the appropriate lesson will be learned. Pray, my friend, always pray.

Experience teaches only the teachable.
- Aldous Huxley -

Be True to You

Those who hope in the Lord will renew their strength.
They will soar on wings like eagles; they will run and
not grow weary, they will walk and not be faint.

- Isaiah 40:31 -

Why? Why would my young daughter behave one way with school friends and another way with church friends and even another way with me? And ... why would she post these things on social media sites and not realize that I will see them? I don't get it. Wait a minute ... OK, I do get it. She wants EVERYONE to like her so she's playing to the audience she is with at any given time. Wow, that's dangerous. It scares me.

How do I help her gain the confidence to know who she is and just be that person? I know it isn't easy. But, I don't want her to forget who she is and to whom she belongs — a commitment she made a long time ago. Help me, God, to help her!

No man, for any considerable period,
can wear one face to himself and
another to the multitude without finally
getting bewildered as to which may be the true.

- Nathaniel Hawthorne -

Courage from God

Be strong and courageous. Do not be terrified;
do not be discouraged, for the Lord your
God will be with you wherever you go.
- Joshua 1:9 -

My son starts school tomorrow. Not a big deal, right? Except this is a brand-new school in a brand-new town where there will be no old friends to greet him and ask about his summer. He's scared and truthfully, I'm a little scared for him. I want to encourage him to be courageous — but in an honest way.

I can't promise that he will make friends right off the bat. I can only pray with him tonight and ask God to help him. I can promise to pray day after day (and I will). I can promise that God will walk with him every step of the way. I can promise that eventually, it will be OK and this place will be home and he will have friends. I can promise that because God led us here. He won't drop us now.

We will both pray our way out of fear and into courage.

Courage is fear that has said its prayers.
- Dorothy Bernard -

Others First

*"I was hungry and you gave Me something to eat,
I was thirsty and you gave Me something drink,
I was a stranger and you invited Me in, I needed
clothes and you clothed Me, I was sick and you looked
after Me. I was in prison and you came to visit Me."*
- Matthew 25:35-36 -

The quote below offers an amazing concept to teach my children — do not befriend people just for what they can do for you but look for what you can do for them. It is such a small thing to give a smile, a helping hand, an encouraging word, an hour of assistance or even a day of help.

I want to help my children learn what a joy it is to know that you've made a difference in someone else's life by your unselfish gift of ... you. I think the best way to help them learn this will be to model it for them. Two blessings! I get to experience the joy of helping someone ... and teach my children something special!

There is no greater joy nor greater reward than to make a fundamental difference in someone's life.
- Sister Mary Rose MacGeady -

With ... not Around

Sons are a heritage from the Lord,
children a reward from Him.
- Psalm 127:3 -

Read the quote for today, Mom. Read it again. Now, read it again. Thank you, Annie Dillard, for a blunt reminder to pay attention. Before we know it, our babies are toddlers, our toddlers are in school, then middle school, high school and boom ... they are out of the house.

How did we spend our days? Busy with careers, cleaning our houses, serving on church committees or pursuing favorite hobbies? Or did we spend our days reading books, playing games, singing silly songs, teaching tender prayers, giggling and hugging ... did we spend them WITH our children and not simply AROUND them?

God entrusted us with these precious children; let's spend our days (and by that our lives) loving and teaching, and loving them some more!

How we spend our days is, of course,
how we spend our lives.
- Annie Dillard -

Second Chances

Not that I have already obtained all this,
or have already been made perfect, but I press
on to take hold of that for which Christ Jesus took
hold of me ... one thing I do: Forgetting what is
behind and straining toward what is ahead, I press
on toward the goal to win the prize for which God
has called me heavenward in Christ Jesus.
- Philippians 3:12-14 -

One of the most intensive exercises I do is ... jumping to conclusions. And ... it always gets me in trouble. Still, I do it over and over — by assuming I know what my teens are up to and sometimes I am waaaayyy off base. You'd think I'd learn my lesson right? You'd think I would wait to get all the information before I leap to a conclusion.

But, I don't and every time I take one of these uninformed leaps, on the way down I think, "Oh yeah, I've been here before. I made this same mistake last week and the week before that and ..." At least now I recognize the mistake. So I ask forgiveness and start again.

Experience is that marvelous thing that enables you
to recognize a mistake when you make it again.
- Franklin P. Jones -

True Contentment

How do you teach a 10-year-old not to envy? Whew ... for that matter how do you teach a 30-something-year-old not to envy? It's hard sometimes when you look around and see those who appear to have an easy life. Those who apparently have few problems, successful careers, lovely homes, nice homes, fun vacations, lots of toys ... OK, this could go on and on.

We moms can spout all the lovely "do not envy" words and even Scripture verses we want but the best way to teach our children not to envy is to model it. Model being happy with what we have — even celebrating it. Model true happiness for those who have more and true compassion for those who have less. Share what we have and enjoy it when others share what they have.

Why do all this? Because, as Solzhenitsyn said, envy can devour us. It can suck the joy right out of our lives. No fun. None at all.

Our envy of others devours us most of all.
- Alexander Solzhenitsyn -

Living through Unfairness

We also rejoice in our sufferings, because we know that suffering produces perseverance; perseverance, character; and character, hope.
- Romans 5:3-4 -

My son came home from school fighting tears ... again. He thinks his teacher has it in for him. When any of my kids have had these kinds of feelings in the past I usually think they are overreacting and being dramatic. But, I have to admit that this time, I pretty much agree with my son.

I've talked to other moms who have kids in his class and they report what their children say about how this teacher treats my son. I've even seen a few instances myself. So, what do I say to my precious son? I tell him the truth — the hard truth. I tell him that yes, he does have a difficult situation and no, he isn't treated fairly. But, God knows and He will use these experiences to make my son stronger and more considerate of others.

Good things can come from tough times.

Every experience God gives us, every person He puts in our lives, is the perfect preparation for the future that only He can see.
- Corrie ten Boom -

Overcoming Cravings

"Ask and it will be given to you; seek and you will find;
knock and the door will be opened to you.
For everyone who asks receives; he who seeks finds;
and to him who knocks, the door will be opened."
- Matthew 7:7-8 -

My daughter struggles with her weight ... an inherited tendency. We've been working on this together; trying to eat balanced meals and take walks and just take better care of ourselves. It's a good thing but not always an easy thing. Both of us respond to stress by craving; I mean CRAVING anything with chocolate.

I've never been prouder of her than when she pulled out the chocolate chip cookies, looked in the bag then closed it and shoved it back into the pantry. She grabbed a piece of fruit and left the kitchen. One chocolate craving at a time, she is teaching herself to overcome and eat more carefully. She prays hard about this and I pray for her ... and for me.

If she can do it, so can I — with God's help!

I count him braver who overcomes his desires
than him who overcomes his enemies.
- Aristotle -

God Is Nearer than You Think

No one will be able to stand up against you all the days of your life. As I was with Moses, so I will be with you; I will never leave you nor forsake you.
- Joshua 1:5 -

I'm scared. I'm hurting. My heart is shouting, "God, where are You? I need to hear Your voice. I need to see Your hand. I need to know that You are aware of what's going on here. I need to know that You have a plan! God, help me. Save me. Protect me!"

Have you ever cried out to God like that ... on your own behalf or on your child's behalf? Have you begged God to step in and change the situation, fix the problem, protect supernaturally?

It may not always "feel" like God is close. It may not always seem that He is handling our problems or even aware of them. But ... He is close. He does know what's going on. He cares more than we can even imagine. He knows our heart's cry before it is even uttered. Thankfully ... He knows.

We need never shout across the spaces to an absent God. He is nearer than our own soul, closer than our most secret thoughts.
- A. W. Tozer -

Precious Children

"For God so loved the world that He gave His one and only Son, that whoever believes in Him shall not perish but have eternal life."
- John 3:16 -

My grandsons are engrossed in their play with their "choo-choos." So busy creating scenes, scripts and situations, they aren't even aware that I'm watching them. They are so precious. I love watching them play. Their innocence and trusting joy of life makes my problems and worries fade away for a moment. Children are truly a gift from God who make me realize afresh His love and care. They are a reminder of the purity and depth of His love.

Some of my favorite moments these days are spent reading to my grandsons, sharing their laughter and enjoying their discoveries of the world. Of course, grandmother mode kicks in, too, and I want to buy them toys and treats, do anything and everything for them. I want them to know how very, very much they are loved.

Hmmm, I'm guessing that may be exactly what my heavenly Father wants me to know about Him, too. Cool.

God sends children to enlarge our hearts, and make us unselfish and full of kindly sympathies and affections.

- Mary Howitt -

Strength Builders

Consider it pure joy, my brothers, whenever you face trials of many kinds, because you know that the testing of your faith develops perseverance.
- James 1:2-3 -

A mother's tendency might be to protect her children from problems in life. I know there was a time when I worked hard at "fixing" things for my daughters, trying to make certain they were always happy. But then I realized that I was not doing them a favor.

How did I realize that? In an exercise program. That's right. You see, in the beginning I was able to lift only 30 pounds but after a few weeks I could lift 65 pounds. That increase came with work, pain, persistence and lots of sweat. But, I'm stronger for it ... and I'm not yet finished. That's when the Scripture verses about trials making our faith stronger actually became a visual for me.

So, I'm not protecting my children all the time anymore but I'm close by with a hug, shoulder to cry on and lots and lots of prayer. They're going to be stronger for their trials and that's a good thing.

Character cannot be developed in ease and quiet. Only through experience of trial and suffering can the soul be strengthened, ambition inspired, and success achieved.
- Helen Keller -

Humble Confidence

*Young men, in the same way be submissive to those
who are older. All of you, clothe yourselves with
humility toward one another, because "God opposes
the proud but gives grace to the humble."*
- 1 Peter 5:5-6 -

Here's my prayer for today:

Dear God, show me how to help my children learn
to be humble with confidence. It isn't an easy thing to
know the line between humility with confidence, and
pride. I want them to know that pride and arrogance
are unattractive and unfriendly characteristics in
anyone. But, I also want them to be confident in who
You made them to be. I want them to trust their
abilities, enjoy their capabilities and happily use them
and grow them.

Of course, they must realize that every talent
and skill they have come from You and plays into
the work You have for them in this life. Help them
discover this truth, God. Help them celebrate who
they are. Help them grow and learn and use their
talents and personalities for You!

Amen.

*Believe in yourself! Have faith in your abilities!
Without a humble but reasonable
confidence in your own powers you
cannot be successful or happy.*

- Norman Vincent Peale -

Grateful Hearts

Give thanks to the Lord, for He is good,
His love endures forever.
- 1 Chronicles 16:34 -

We all know we're supposed to be thankful, right? And yes, we say we are thankful for the many blessings God has heaped upon us. Actually though, true, heartfelt gratitude explodes from our hearts only after we stop and think about past failures and the forgiveness that followed; past hopelessness followed by surprise blessings.

Gratitude that is deep and true comes once we realize how little we "deserve" and how generous God is in love and care. True gratitude is a response to that. What a gift to share with our children. As we encourage them to notice how generous God is to them and to give Him credit for the blessings in their lives, real gratitude will flow from them. What a great way to live!

Gratitude is born in hearts that take
time to count up past mercies.
- Charles E. Jefferson -

Scared Straight

Serve the Lord with fear
and rejoice with trembling.
- Psalm 2:11 -

I tell my teens to be careful about who they spend their time with. I tell them that friends can have an influence on how they spend their time, the choices they make, and the values they adopt. I tell them. Do they listen to me? Not always.

What makes an impression on them is when one of the friends they choose to hang out with gets in trouble. When my kids realize how close they came to getting in trouble themselves ... well, then they become more willing to listen.

It's difficult to let my kids learn lessons the hard way and of course I would protect them if they were in real danger, but the truth is that lessons they learn the hard way — through a good scare — make a big impression and will not be quickly forgotten ... by either of us.

A good scare is more effective than good advice.
- Anonymous -

The Power of Words

I long to help my children understand how deeply their unkind, thoughtless words can hurt another person. My daughter has the sharpest tongue. Her words are sometimes so cutting and harsh. I've seen the pangs of hurt flash across her siblings' faces at her hurtful comments. I've seen her friends turn and walk away from her. I've felt the sting of her words myself.

How do I help my daughter understand that the unkind words she spouts remain in the hearts of those she hurts, damaging self-esteem, friendships and lives? One way I can help her see what she is doing is to be careful myself of the words I speak and the tone I use. Because, truth be told, I see a lot of myself in my daughter. Perhaps she learned her harshness from me. So, I'll change me (with God's help) and encourage my daughter to change, too.

No sword bites so fiercely as an evil tongue.
- Sir Philip Sidney -

Faith in the Dark

*Praise be to the God and Father of our Lord Jesus
Christ, the Father of compassion and the God of
all comfort, who comforts us in our troubles, so that
we can comfort those in any trouble with the
comfort we ourselves have received from God.*
- 2 Corinthians 1:3-4 -

The day is bright and sunny. My marriage is
good. My kids are wonderful. I feel great! It's easy to
trust God when things in life are going well. We sing
praises, pray prayers, speak of how wonderful God
is. But, what happens when life gets difficult — when
relationships are broken, health is taken away, jobs
are lost, kids rebel ... when life happens? How does
my faith handle that?

The thing is that I only really need faith when life
gets a little dark. If I truly trust God and believe that
He honestly loves me I won't turn away from Him
when things get difficult. It is in the dark days of life
that I have the opportunity to see God's love and
care in action. Trust and faith gives the opportunity.

*Faithless is he that says farewell
when the road darkens.*
- J. R. R. Tolkien -

Get Busy!

"Look at the birds of the air; they do not sow or reap or store away in barns, and yet your heavenly Father feeds them. Are you not much more valuable than they? Who of you by worrying can add a single hour to his life?"
- Matthew 6:26-27 -

My husband lost his job. I'm scared. How will we pay the mortgage? How will we provide food for our family? How will we make it? I know a lot of people are in the same position we are ... but it is different when it's personal.

My heart is pulled back to my trust that God is in control. He knows what has happened. He isn't surprised by it and He will take care of us. I want to be an example to my children of what it looks like to trust God in scary times. So, each time I take a deep breath I exhale a prayer for the courage to hang on.

My husband and I will join hands and hearts and get creative in taking care of our family. We'll do our part because we know that God will do His.

You can't wring your hands and roll up your sleeves at the same time.
- Pat Schroeder -

Caring for Others

Two are better than one, because they have
a good return for their work: If one falls down,
his friend can help him up. But pity the man
who falls and has no one to help him up!
- Ecclesiastes 4:9-10 -

My husband got a job promotion! This is great news for him ... more money; new challenges; more responsibility. He's excited and I'm excited for him. However, this means we're moving; not only to a new town but to a new state! I'm excited about that but my three kids ... not so much. They are sad about leaving their friends and are very anxious about making new friends in our new town.

My heart aches for my kids and I long to help them see the adventure of this new opportunity. I pray for the wisdom to be able to teach them about ways to get to know people — ask questions, show interest in others' lives and their likes and hobbies. Make other people feel important. Well, I know I need to listen to my own advice. We'll move. We'll miss our old friends. We will make new ones. An adventure!

You can make more friends in two months
by becoming interested in other people
than you can in two years by trying to
get other people interested in you.
- Dale Carnegie -

The Change in Me

*And we, who with unveiled faces all reflect the
Lord's glory, are being transformed into His
likeness with ever-increasing glory, which comes
from the Lord, who is the Spirit.*
- 2 Corinthians 3:18 -

I will admit it. I'm guilty of spending a lot of time and effort trying to change everyone around me so that they will think as I do and value what I value. After all, life would be much easier (and more peaceful) if everyone agreed with me!

However, the older I get the more obvious it becomes that perhaps it could be the case that once in a while it might be me who needs to change. It's revolutionary to think that I am not always right. This is especially difficult in relation to my children. I cannot mold any one of them into a little "me" and I guess I shouldn't even want to.

Instead, my goal for me, as well as for each of my children, should be that we each become more Christlike. That should be MY goal and the truth is that to become that kind of woman, well, I need to do some changing, for sure!

*Everyone thinks of changing the world,
but no one thinks of changing himself.*
- Leo Tolstoy -

Keep On Keepin' On!

Therefore, if anyone is in Christ, he is a new creation;
the old has gone, the new has come!
- 2 Corinthians 5:17 -

Life is about growth and change. Even if I don't want to grow and change; I need to. I see in my children how they are "keeping up with the times" by learning about technology and adapting to changes in how we live and communicate with one another. I need to learn from them — I know I'm a good communicator. But, I want to communicate in my own way and style and I am not keeping up with the times.

So, if I want to keep up with the times and stay in touch with people young and old — I need to keep moving, learning and growing. Otherwise, life may pass me by. I don't want to wake up one morning and realize that I'm ... old. I mean old in how I think and behave and in how I relate to others. I'm sure my children will help me. They love showing me how much more they know than I!

Even if you're on the right track,
you'll get run over if you just sit there.
- Will Rogers -

Showing My
Kids How

I have set the Lord always before me.
Because He is at my right hand, I will not be shaken.
Therefore my heart is glad and my tongue rejoices;
my body also will rest secure.
- Psalm 16:8-9 -

There are some experiences and some times in life that simply stink — I mean they ARE NOT fun. Broken relationships, financial strains, health issues, job stresses ... things that go on and on and make it hard for us to get up in the morning and face another day of the same kinds of things.

These are not fun times to talk about. What makes it even harder is that some people say that because we are Christians we should not admit to having negative feelings. We should trust God and give glory to Him. Of course that is true. It is also true that God helps us through the difficult times. One of the ways He does this is through our children. We get up to face another day because our children need to see us do that. They need to see the reality of our faith in difficult times.

Children are the anchors that hold a mother to life.
- Sophocles -

Silly Songs

My daughter has a friend who has everything. Seriously, this girl has every toy imaginable. Whatever she wants shows up in a day or two ... every item of clothing, every vacation ... everything. It's hard to keep up with and actually difficult to even find things to get her for birthday parties.

At one time I wondered if my daughter was jealous of this friend who is showered with "stuff." But, not long ago my fears were put to rest when my daughter hugged me and told me how special I make her feel. I don't buy her a lot of stuff, but I love being with her and talking with her. We laugh. We sing silly songs. We brainstorm things she might do when she grows up.

What a joy to know that she loves these times as much as me.

Children will not remember you for
the material things you provided but
for the feeling that you cherished them.
- Richard L. Evans -

The Fog Clears

Know therefore that the Lord your God is God;
He is the faithful God, keeping His covenant
of love to a thousand generations of those
who love Him and keep His commands.
- Deuteronomy 7:9 -

I remember driving home from a friend's house one night when the fog was so thick that the headlights of my car showed only whiteness ahead of me. Not one inch of the road was illuminated. I couldn't see where I was going or where I had been. It was very disconcerting because there were no reference points to help me know if I was even on the road or to warn me of what might lie ahead.

Life is like that sometimes, isn't it? Everything is lost in a fog and we can't find any reference points, any landmarks. That's when faith becomes reality. Faith in our God who loves us and guides us through the fog, bringing us to a point where we can see again. Faith is the only reference point we need.

Faith is like radar that sees through the fog.
- Corrie ten Boom -

True Forgiveness

"If your brother sins, rebuke him, and if he repents,
forgive him. If he sins against you seven times
in a day, and seven times comes back to
you and says, 'I repent,' forgive him."
- Luke 17:3-4 -

My three-year-old grandson has a simple answer to the question, "Why did you hit your brother?" His response is, "Well ... he hit me ... on purpose!" He hasn't learned the process of forgiveness yet. But, we're working on it.

Forgiveness is giving up the need to get even. It's realizing that there is a chance that the hurt inflicted on you was not intentional. Forgiveness is deciding that even if the first strike was intentional, forgiveness is a better route than all-out battle! The strength to forgive makes you stronger than the one who must always get even.

OK, this is a great thing to know and it's not too early to begin teaching it to a three-year-old. It's not going to be easy though, and I may get to show examples of what forgiveness looks like along the way. Good exercise for me!

Forgiveness is me giving up the right
to hurt you for hurting me.
- Anonymous -

Compassionate Living

*Because of the Lord's great love we are not consumed,
for His compassions never fail. They are new
every morning; great is your faithfulness.*
- Lamentations 3:22-23 -

The quote below leads my mind right to the Bible verse that tells us that faith without action is dead. What good is it to know the definition of the word *compassion* if it doesn't show in my life? This is a core thing I want to teach my children ... knowing Bible verses is not enough. The ability to rattle off the Ten Commandments is not enough. Being able to describe Jesus' interaction with people is not enough.

The evidence of Christ's presence in our lives is when the head knowledge flows through our hearts and into action. Compassion makes a difference in how we relate to other people only when we can show it — not define it. I believe my children will more easily and quickly reflect Christ to those around them when they make the journey from knowledge to action.

*I would rather feel compassion
than know the meaning of it.*
- Thomas Aquinas -

Heart of Love

Do everything without complaining or arguing, so that you may become blameless and pure, children of God without fault in a crooked and depraved generation, in which you shine like stars in the universe.
- Philippians 2:14-15 -

You possibly know at least one person who is seldom, if ever, happy. A person who constantly complains and consistently sees the proverbial glass as half empty, never half full. Oh my, that sort of person is tiring. She can drain the joy right out of your own life. It's especially draining when this person is a member of your own family.

What makes a person become so negative; so unhappy? One pathway to negativity is a lack of love. That would be a lack of love for others and a lack of love for self. Because seriously, when your heart is filled with love for others, is it really possible to be completely negative? Nope. Love begets joy: love for God; love for others; love for self.

A joyful heart is the inevitable result of a heart burning with love.
- Mother Teresa -

You Can't Win without Trying

David also said to Solomon his son, "Be strong and courageous, and do the work. Do not be afraid or discouraged, for the LORD God, my God, is with you. He will not fail you or forsake you until all the work for the service of the temple of the LORD is finished."
- 1 Chronicles 28:20 -

My six-year-old son is afraid to fail. His first grade teacher just reported to me that he is afraid to try reading out loud. He is nervous about addition and subtraction. He refuses to try new sports. None of these fears have foundation in lack of ability ... only in fear of failure. There is such a high value placed on winning these days that the perfectionist children of our world are afraid to fail.

But, if my son never tries new things he will not know the joy of learning new things or of succeeding. He will simply have never failed. Failure is not where any of us want to be, but we can take our failures and learn from them. Winning is great fun but failure is a great teacher!

Next to trying and winning the next best thing is trying and failing.
- Lucy Maud Montgomery -

Sticking with It!

As you know, we consider blessed those who have persevered. You have heard of Job's perseverance and have seen what the Lord finally brought about. The Lord is full of compassion and mercy.

- James 5:11 -

"I can't do it. It's too hard. It takes too long!" How many times have you heard your children say these words or something like them? OK, honesty time — how many times have you at least thought them to yourself? These words might have been your response to anything from losing weight to reading through the Bible. Whatever task was before you, it seemed too big to handle.

A practical lesson for your children (and for you) is that any task is doable if it is broken down into segments you can handle. Set small goals, and make a work chart that breaks the big task into smaller jobs that you can manage. If you can do this, and teach your children to do it, they will learn perseverance — sticking with a job until it's done. That's a great life skill!

Perseverance is not a long race;
it is many short races one after the other.

- Walter Elliot -

True Thankfulness

Let the peace of Christ rule in your hearts,
since as members of one body you were
called to peace. And be thankful.
- Colossians 3:15 -

My daughter has a case of the "I wants ... " Perhaps you know what I'm talking about. She wants everything she sees; everything she hears about. It doesn't stop with "stuff" either. She wants me to serve her, help her, take care of her. She wants. She wants. She wants. You get the idea. This is disturbing enough but adding to my annoyance is the fact that she seldom says a simple "thank you." A thank you should not be so difficult.

Wow. I wonder if God sometimes feels this way? My prayers are filled with what I want and I even tell Him how to do it ... and when He should do it. When I think of the multitude of blessing He has showered on me, then this quotation hits home — saying thank you, especially to God, goes a long, long way, plus my children will learn from my example!

If the only prayer you ever say in your
whole life is "thank you," it will be enough.
- Meister Eckhart -

Stay True to *You*

Why do teenagers care so much about what other kids think of them? It's so important to "fit in." My teenage daughter's concern for others' opinions keeps me on my knees; that's for sure! She wants to have a reputation that keeps her with the "in crowd" so I constantly pray that she doesn't compromise her own values and beliefs to attain that reputation. I know she was raised well with good morals, good values and a foundation in God's Word.

As my daughter matures she will learn that it is more important to stay true to who she is and thus to think well of herself. Sacrificing herself in order to be accepted by others will only make her unhappy with the person she becomes. In the end, she will more than likely find that thinking well of herself will lead to being well thought of by others; at least by the others who really matter.

A good reputation is being well thought of;
a good conscience is thinking well of yourself.
- William A. Ward -

Sunbeams!

Because He Himself suffered when He was tempted,
He is able to help those who are being tempted.
- Hebrews 2:18 -

Sometimes the tendency when a situation gets difficult is to give up, pull back or walk away. Sometimes we even spiritualize our actions by saying that God put up these roadblocks so He must not want us to move forward. Perhaps we should consider that He may just want us to persevere — to push our way through the difficulties until we see the success.

What if we thought about difficulties like a cloud-filled sky through which no beam of sunlight could be seen? But, suddenly, without warning, we see the light of the sun fighting its way through the clouds until a small beam breaks through. The rewards and lessons of pushing through difficulties can barely be measured — and are not to be missed!

In the middle of difficulty lies opportunity.
- Albert Einstein -

Using Money Wisely

A generous man will himself be blessed,
for he shares his food with the poor.
- Proverbs 22:9 -

The world feeds us (and our children) an insistent message that what makes a person successful is the ability to earn lots and lots of money. There is certainly nothing wrong with earning a lot of money, but there is a responsibility in the proper way to spend it and a way to honor God through it.

What is that? Give it away. Help those who are less fortunate or who have lived through a natural disaster and lost everything they own, including a way to feed and clothe themselves and their children.

The goal is to share what God has blessed you with. Pay attention to the people in our world who must get by on pennies a day; people who watch their children die of starvation or exposure. Help them by sharing what God has blessed you with.

Make all you can,
save all you can,
give all you can.
- John Wesley -

Living on the B-Team

I am convinced that neither death nor life, neither angels nor demons, neither the present nor the future, nor any powers, neither height nor depth, nor anything else in all creation, will be able to separate us from the love of God that is in Christ Jesus our Lord.

- Romans 8:38-39 -

"B-team! I only made the B-team! That's like first loser team!" my son moaned. I could sense his self-esteem nose-diving with each word he spoke. "No one even comes to the games!"

"I'll be at every game," I assured him.

"You HAVE to come. You're my mom!" He threw these words over his shoulder as he stormed out of the room.

Well, I kind of understand how my son feels. There have been times when I've felt like I live on a B-team — especially where God is concerned. There have been times when it feels like answering my prayers is a job that is way down on His to-do list — down at B-team level. Reminders that He loves me like no other are exactly what I need to hear.

God loves each of us as if there were only one of us.

- St. Augustine -

Teach, Love, Pray

But be sure to fear the Lord and
serve Him faithfully with all your heart;
consider what great things He has done for you.
- 1 Samuel 12:24 -

I've heard several young women say that they feel their lives are on hold because their hours, days and weeks are consumed with being mommies.

There is no doubt that motherhood is a 24-hour-a-day job! Because of this, many of us wonder how we're supposed to find time to serve God. After all, our days are consumed with runny noses, dirty diapers, mac-'n cheese and play dates.

But, what does it mean to "serve God?" I would never bemoan the privilege of motherhood, but how does it fit in with serving God? That is answered when I watch my sweet babies sleeping and I realize that there really isn't anything more important than teaching, loving and praying for these precious ones. I AM serving God right now, every day by being a conscientious and loving mother.

God makes three requests of His children:
Do the best you can, where you are,
with what you have, now.
- African-American Proverb -

Working for Change

*Anyone, then, who knows the good
he ought to do and doesn't do it, sins.*
- James 4:17 -

I have daughters. Precious, beautiful, innocent daughters. I would do anything for them. Anything. My husband and I provide food, clothing and a home for them. We teach them so they can become productive members of society. We protect them. We love them. I hear stories of human trafficking, forced prostitution and all kinds of horrible things that happen to other parents' daughters.

It's a temptation to say, "Well, those things happen in other parts of the world, not here." But ... it shouldn't matter if these things happen here or on the other side of the world. It must be stopped! People say that "someone" has to do something and I agree. But, even in my agreeing I know that someone has to be that "someone."

Nothing will change if individuals do not take a stand and make an effort to stop the atrocities. Maybe God is calling me to be the "someone" ... to do what I can and make a difference in my part of the world.

*All that is necessary for evil to succeed
is that good men do nothing.*
- Edmund Burke -

Who Is in Charge?

*God placed all things under His feet and
appointed Him to be head over everything for
the church, which is His body, the fullness of
Him who fills everything in every way.*
- Ephesians 1:22-23 -

I have control issues, OK? I know that, and even if I didn't know it, my children are happy to point it out to me ... often. I'm a mom and I've spent my whole mom career protecting my children, guiding their choices of activities and friends. I've prayed for them, taught them, helped them. And now they are young adults and I'm still trying to run their lives. At least that's what they say.

It's just that I love them so much. I care about what happens to them and OK, maybe sometimes I try to influence their actions and choices. They say that sometimes I try to play God. I don't mean to, though. And actually, realizing that there is a God — and it isn't me — does take the pressure off.

The best thing I can do for my children is to pray for them, listen to them, love them and let God take care of them!

*For peace of mind, resign as
general manager of the universe.*

- Anonymous -

Model Living

*In everything set them an example by doing what
is good. In your teaching show integrity, seriousness.*
- Titus 2:7 -

"How many times do I have to tell you this?" I sigh. My child has ONCE AGAIN broken a familiar rule or perhaps he has once again left his clothes all over the floor or hurt his brother. Whatever the offense, I know I've told him about a gazillion times not to do it! Seriously, sometimes it feels like I'm talking to a brick wall! Why doesn't my son just listen?

The reality is we can talk to our children until we're blue in the face. But, our children will learn more about good behavior by watching how we live; not by hearing what we say. Phew, that puts the pressure on us, doesn't it? Moms, we need to "walk the talk" in order to teach our children. We show that the things we try to teach our children are really important by incorporating those things into our lives.

*Children have never been very good
at listening to their elders, but they
have never failed to imitate them.*
- James Arthur Baldwin -

Childlike Forgiveness

*"Forgive us our debts, as we also
have forgiven our debtors."*
- Matthew 6:12 -

Aaarrrggghhh!!! I did it again. I totally lost my cool with my children today. I lost my temper and shouted at them. Yes, they were disobedient and yes, they were fighting with one another, but I really should have been a bit cooler in my response. After all, I'm the adult so I should be in control and act ... like an adult.

Now, once again, I must apologize to them. I must ask forgiveness and promise to try harder to never lose control again. They will forgive me. They always do. Of course, I will ask, they will forgive, and then this process will happen again. Right at this moment in time, I'm very thankful for my children's forgiving hearts. They will forgive me and go right on loving me.

Children are so good at modeling the forgiveness and love of God. They do it much better than adults do. Yes, I'm thankful. So thankful.

*No one forgives with more
grace and love than a child.*
- Anonymous -

Healing Laughter

You have made known to me the path of life;
You will fill me with joy in Your presence,
with eternal pleasures at Your right hand.
- Psalm 16:11 -

I read a book to my children tonight. We do that pretty much every night. But, tonight in the middle of the story, one of my kids got the giggles. She laughed and laughed until finally all of us were laughing. We rolled around on the couch, laughing until tears rolled down our cheeks. It was a precious, memory-making time made even more special by the fact that we had had a tough day together, one of those days when the kids were obstinate and mom was short on patience.

When we sat down with the book none of us were especially happy to be together. But the laughter washed away all the bad feelings. By the end of our giggles all the negativity was pushed back and our love for one another was right in front — where it should be. Thank God for laughter!

What soap is to the body, laughter is to the soul.
- Yiddish Proverb -

Golden Rule Living

"So in everything, do to others what you would have them do to you, for this sums up the Law and the Prophets."
- Matthew 7:12 -

You know the Golden Rule. You've probably quoted it to your children dozens of times with the explanation of, "You wouldn't want your brother to do that to you, would you?" It makes so much sense to adults, doesn't it? Living out the standards of the Golden Rule is a great way to live — in fact, a necessary way to get along with others.

However, I wonder how often we apply the Golden Rule to our children's relationships with one another, but neglect to apply it to our own? Are we careful to treat our children as we would like them to treat us? Do we show them the respect and consideration that we expect? Do we treat them as well as we treat other adults? Living out the Golden Rule is the best way to teach it!

We have committed the Golden Rule to memory. Let us now commit it to life.
- Edwin Markham -

What Really Matters

Do not be anxious about anything, but in everything,
by prayer and petition, with thanksgiving,
present your requests to God.
- Philippians 4:6 -

Are you a world-class worrier? Perhaps you try not to worry but it keeps creeping back into your heart. Worry is like water that rolls around, searching for the place it can sneak in and do damage.

Of course, Christians are not SUPPOSED to worry. We trust God. We give our problems to Him. But, it seems that many women are plagued by the "what ifs" for ourselves and our families. We try not to worry about what could happen or what might happen ... but sometimes, in the middle of the night, we are sleepless in the land of worry.

The thing about worry is that our energy is often expended on things that never happen and if we could get a grasp on our emotions, we would know they are not likely to happen. So, our energy, thought time, emotions and even desperate prayers are spent on imaginary troubles. What a waste.

If I had my life to live over,
I would perhaps have more actual troubles
but I'd have fewer imaginary ones.
- Don Herold -

Using What We've Got

*"Whoever wants to be first must be slave of all.
For even the Son of Man did not come to be served,
but to serve, and to give His life as a ransom for many."*
- Mark 10:44-45 -

Thank You, God, for the unique interests, talents and gifts You give to each of us. Thank You that as we're busy being wives, mothers, daughters, siblings, employees and volunteers we are using up those gifts You've given us. Thank You that the more we pour out, the more you refill. Thank You that for as long as our minds and bodies can function on this planet there are ways we can serve You.

I echo the words of Ms. Bombeck below with the prayer that I never stop serving, giving and loving. I pray for the strength to keep going forward in the face of discouragement, exhaustion and confusion. I pray for the ability to keep my eyes focused on Jesus and the understanding of the privilege of serving Him. I pray to use all things You've given me for all the time You've given me.

*When I stand before God at the end of my life,
I would hope that I would not have a
single bit of talent left, and could say,
"I used everything You gave me."*
- Erma Bombeck -

Opportunity in Crisis

If we know that He hears us – whatever we ask –
we know that we have what we asked of Him.
- 1 John 5:15 -

Does it sometimes seem that your life bounces from one crisis to the next? After a while you start to feel like you live in a pinball machine, right? It's tiring. It's discouraging. It seems endless. The tendency is to close the curtains, turn out the lights and lie down in the darkness and stay there so long that you slide past the rest-and-rejuvenation stage to the giving-up stage. You don't want to work to get out of the pit you're in or fight for survival.

However, the quote below by John F. Kennedy is an eye-opener. Can there really be opportunity in crisis? Of course there can, but seeing problems as opportunities is a choice you make – with prayer. You can (and should) pray diligently about your crisis. But, are most of those prayers requests for God to solve the problem or take it away altogether? Perhaps your prayers should be for God to show you the opportunity in the crisis.

When written in Chinese, the word crisis *is composed of two characters – one represents danger and the other represents opportunity.*
- John F. Kennedy -

Wasting Energy

"You have heard that it was said, 'Love your neighbor and hate your enemy.' But I tell you: Love your enemies and pray for those who persecute you."
- Matthew 5:43-44 -

I can take a lot of things in this life but one thing that gets my ire up is when someone hurts one of my children. Recently — a good friend (I thought) did something that really hurt my kids. Whether it was intentional or not, I don't really know. But I'm sorry to admit that my response was anger. I wasted a lot of time and energy on the one-sided mental arguments we humans have at 2 AM.

You do know what I'm talking about, right ... the arguments the other person doesn't even know about but we always win? My friend didn't get to participate in the argument and perhaps didn't even know how angry and hurt I was. OK, I didn't hate her, but a lot of energy was wasted on the bad feelings I had — what a waste.

A much better solution ... talk to my friend. Find out what really happened ... or ... just let it go and move on.

Hating people is like burning down your own house to get rid of a rat.
- Harry Emerson Fosdick -

Other Books in the
GodMoments series

GodMoments for Women

GodMoments for Men

GodMoments for You